IntroVersations

~

*Conversations between an introvert
and, of course, himself.*

To Emmy (Milena), who has patiently walked with me and believes in these words perhaps even more than I do.

~

And for Dad, whose encouragement
--tangibly and intangibly--
helped to pen many of these poems.

Contents

Introduction   **6**
Found Poetry   **9**
Warmwind   12
Whether   13
Drink Up   14
Come Thin Morning   15
Half Smile   16
Sour Gas   17
That Outside   18
Faster & Louder   19
The Lies   20
Work To Worry   21
Intentional Poetry   **23**
No One Else Around   25
Who I Am   27
Awhile   29
A-Z-A Again   31
In The Affirmative   33
in//exhale   35
In Loving Memory of Me   37
Delusions   39
(Cheap, Free Pardon)
Escapes   43
In You We Become   45
Surely   47

Desire   51
Lady Wisdom Cries   53
The Harlot   57
I've Been   61
Closed   65
First   67
I, Mystery   69
Breath   71
Inclined   75
Shut Up   77
Still   79
Exist   81
Juxtaposed   83
Closed Tight   85
Never Live Again   87
Reminisce   89
The Place That Never Ends   91
Disappointment   93
Tears   97
Rain Today   99
Everstill   101
Glass   103
Paradox   105
Shadows   107
In & Out   109

Introduction

As an introvert, I generally have a lot going on inside my head.

Not that extroverts *don't* have a lot going on...

It's just that usually, whatever *they* have going on is going on *outside* of their head, where everyone else can see it, interact with it, and hold it up in high esteem as something to be striven for...

Me?

As I've said, most of it is going on *inside* my head, away from everyone else...and it only occasionally is allowed to see the light of day.

It's not because it's something particularly terrible or anything, or because I'm ashamed of the things that run through my head-- it's simply that I'm not as naturally inclined to share them outwardly, openly, or in group settings.

It doesn't matter that I've learned to be happy with my "voice" in my writing, and it doesn't matter that I've received positive reinforcement and glowing comments from both people who know me and are complete strangers, alike.

It's not a matter of not being willing to share—it's literally a lack of natural inclination, as noted above. So unless I've decided to commit to something, and get those thoughts out in the open, they generally stay in, and spend a lot of time mulling around in, my head.

To me, poetry has always been a matter of conversation. Whoever is writing is attempting to converse with the reader in a way which will inspire and ignite a picture, a feeling, an idea, which then takes on a life of its own. Poetry often plumbs the depths of our human experience, and as such carries with it a "realness" and unafraid quality which doesn't tend to shy away from any subject, so long as it falls within the scope of the poet's imagination and experience. Poetry is not afraid to face demons or angels, religion or politics, fears or joys, highs or lows. It is not afraid to make utter, logical sense, or to be complete gibberish, in the pursuit of communicating what it must.

Poetry, in my mind, is also a bit of a fluid category: some of what may traditionally be considered to be "prose" or "freeform", is, to me, poetry, *if it achieves* the goal of painting a picture in the mind's eye of the reader, and emotionally stirring them in some way. Therefore, I have read entire novels which I would consider to be poetry; I've read articles which could be considered verse; I've read pieces in almost any genre of literature which *could* be classified dually as whatever they are *and* poetry—so beautiful is the depth of their words. So if you find, within these pages, something which does not fit the traditional category of "poetry" in your mind—be open to the way the words speak, and, perhaps, find yourself surprised.

In being a deeply personal form of writing, it feels a bit akin to sharing one's journal entries—allowing others in to the conversations and arguments that happen inside of your head.
The observations.
The irritations.
The questions and doubts.
The assurances and faiths.
Poetry, then, is a matter of the writer sharing themselves in a way that many people never do.

Especially introverts.

Which is why I, an introvert, have decided to make that commitment, take that plunge, and allow you in on my "Introversations"--the introverted conversations that run around in my head. My thoughts, my imaginings, my observations, and questions...these are a collection of the diversity that is me.

I have decided to divide this book into two sections: "Found Poetry", and "Intentional Poetry".

"Found Poetry" is poetry that happened (or happens) almost by accident—whether through magnetic poetry on the refrigerator, a small phrase or word that ran away on itself, or a random writing exercise gone right. To me, found poetry is fun, unique, and doesn't necessarily always make sense—except that *no matter what*, it *still communicates* somehow, even if it seems, on the surface, to be complete gibberish or nonsense. It doesn't necessarily seek to speak a truth, or communicate a thought, other than the truth that words are beautiful, living things, and they carry with themselves all sorts of thoughts, imagery, and creative potential. Let your mind run free with these, and see what pictures the words paint on the canvas of your imagination.

"Intentional Poetry", then, would be poetry which I set out to write with intention—to communicate a thought, probe a question, or create a specific image in the mind of the reader. Intentional poetry tends to wrestle, engage, and attempt to unravel thought. It can be much more raw, truthful, and intimate. It tends to be the poetry that engages the emotion and the deeper parts of who we are, and doesn't shy away from asking something of the reader. Much of my intentional poetry stems from times of personal reflection, silence, or focused thought; as I process life, and try to understand how I fit in to the world around me.

Please tread (and read) carefully, and allow the words to melt in the mouth of your mind...to whisper to the ears of your heart, and to open the eyes of your imagination in new, fun, and exciting ways.

--Samuel Geleynse
Kelowna, BC
January, 2016

Found Poetry

~

The random gibberish and nonsense that, somehow,
manages to speak something even without clear direction.

Warmwind

Until gently blew the warm wind,
Cool current lingered, loud
Here testing favour;
Questioning
The things that fit,
The new,
The proud;
Now factor bad alongside good;
An ounce of drink is cheap...
Result?
Divide the plural love
Through printed poverty.

Whether

Whether children travel down the road
Or snow paper the ground once more
Expect an hour of black, sent sound
A diamond only dark can smell

Drink Up

Some simple week
Save one moment;

A comma
In a spreading year

Slow,
Rather than late
It sails;

A ship of sudden rest

Drink up grand lady, boy, mi'lad
'Fore danger pound its chord
And dreadful lake grow very cold
Singular o'er its soil

Come Thin Morning

Each word that climbs upon the edge
Must either method or madness feel
Or syllable;
The match that's struck
To light or heat the paper soul

For several wild men sell the tone;
The rhythm that died long ago
Where oceans sometimes,
Often,
Go

                                    alone.

Explain this last objective sum,
And shout the melody that's gone,
But—

Come thin morning,
Let's discuss
The reason
Order
Matters
Much.

Half Smile

Half smile

    Quiet power

        Hidden door

            Surprise hold

    Strange light

        Written life

                Questions remain
                After winter's long stay

Sour Gas

Success requires
Hard clear methods,
Change of nature,
Every inch

But, should mem'ry
Cough and sputter
Questions grow from
Verdant soil:

Equal parts experience
Young knowledge
And sour gas.

Ever wonder which might prove truest?

That Outside

Ever wonder which might prove true?
You or me or me or you
Perhaps a smile could mark the tone
Me or you or tried and true?
Weighted ever;
Caught and cold
Truth or fiction, fact or fear?
Stand exact now; chance or plan?

"Think thorough thoughts, though, through and through!"

Wonder which one might prove true?
That outside of me and you.

Faster & Louder

Anyone busily splashing asleep
Wanted, attempted, attended, and cheap
Eventually,
Pregnant—
Upsetting the joy

--Remaining--
(pause here and count to four)

So anything, anything
But the stuck hour
Is watching and knocking
Faster and louder

The Lies

Remembering the fickle promise
Communication otherwise denies

Grinning here into the cursed waters
And repeating, too, the lies

Work To Worry

Written in gold since they were past
Whose reach is wide and sharp
While multiplication strains its neck
And rears its head to bark;
Against the lie
Accept the why
With meter—
Slip, and sing!

Just sail direct and board against.
'Gainst almost anything.

Contrast condition,
Quick and small
Watch it fall apart
When you're done,
You've burnt the fun,
Turned work to worry once more

Intentional Poetry

~

The words which paint a picture
of the thoughts inside my life...

This was one of the first poems I ever wrote.
In high school, I used my writing to come to grips with
everything that was going on in life, and to attempt to
reconcile it in my mind, or with
the world I was seeing around me.
While most of my early attempts at poetry were quite
awkward and halting (or even downright embarrassing!),
there were a few that I am not ashamed
to share with people today.
This is one of those poems.

No One Else Around

Laying outside, breeze
　　blowing
a swallow flies over
wings flapping intermittently...

no clouds in sight.

blue continues forever, now
　　another swallow
the sound of chickadees
silence broken
only by them
　　the crickets
and the faint sound of driving cars

somewhere...

not here.

now another swallow
time to think
　　and be alone
just observe
and come to grips
with who I am with no one else around.

"Who I Am" is the sister, or follow-up, poem to
"No One Else Around".
While not written on the same day, or directly in connection
with the other, I penned these words several months down
the road—the next time I tried
my hand at this "poetry" thing.
I remember being satisfied that things seemed to take shape
better than they had in the past,
only to be disappointed the next time I tried to write,
as my thoughts came out clumsy and awkward again, as
they had many times in the past.
It was shortly after writing this poem that I came to realize
that you are never, as a writer,
going to be entirely happy with everything you write.
It just isn't possible.

Who I Am

Outside flat on my back again
but this time there are clouds
      no swallows now
but a wind blows in the trees

the crickets hum on
and all I can do is listen.
The setting sun is so bright
that even if I wanted to look
(which I don't—closed eyes are wonderful)
I wouldn't see much else

but the sky, the sun, the clouds

this reflection
a part of who I am
      moments of silence
are who I am inside
calm, reflective, quiet

loving who I'm made to be.

During my early twenties, I spent about 4 years in a fairly serious depression. Things seemed extremely dark to me, and I gave up on just about everything that I knew I loved to do.
The things that I knew deep down inside to be true of myself no longer mattered to me, and I spent little or no time pursuing my passions because I had no drive to do anything.
One day, I ran across the Apostle Paul's words to the Corinthian church, in 1 Corinthians 13:9-12.
This poem came out of my heart in a moment—in a way that I didn't realize was still capable of writing. This was the first time in probably 3 years I had written any form of poetry whatsoever, and it most certainly took me by surprise.

Awhile

As I am fully known;
So shall I fully know.
While now I see in part,
Then I shall know your heart for me
Here I reflect but dimly
The light your face relays
In wholeness and unbroken love
I'll show your saving grace.

Little one, let's put away
Everything that binds
Let's chase away and break the chains
Of childish reasoning's lies
Each and every moment
Fix your gaze into my eyes
And be transformed by

        resting

     here

          a while.

This poem was really more of an exercise, born out of curiosity, than it was anything else.
I was thinking and reading, and the word "alive" kept coming up, again and again.
I decided to look up different words, in the thesaurus, which meant "alive",
so I could explore the depth of the word a little further, and flesh out my understanding.
This was the result.

A-Z-A Again

Abide, be found, exist, have being;
Be, bide, breathe, dwell, carry on.
Continue, hold,
Draw breath, prevail;
    Walk the earth,
  Inhabit,
Last.

Maintain, remain, reside, sustain.
        Figure in, stand, stay, pertain.

 Keep,
                    Persist,
            Occupy,
      Thrive:

 Live
–Zoetically–
Alive.

I've always found the power of words to be astounding.
In what is perhaps a coincidental irony, it is often the
smallest words that hold,
within themselves, the most unbelievable depth and power.
Think of when a child first discovers
the power of the word "no".
To me, though, perhaps due to my personality,
"yes" is possibly the most frightening
word in our entire language.
It holds the power to overcommit,
to change the course of your life forever,
to betray, condemn, point fingers,
agree, bless, support, admit, or repent.
Such a simple word—such a heavy range of meaning.

In The Affirmative

We dread the words
That shape our lives
Because they hold
Such power
"I Love You"
Or
"We need to talk"
Have robbed brave men
Of courage
The words we speak
Change time and space
"You're worthless" will
Undo you
But I've never met
A more frightening phrase
Than a simply spoken
"Yes"

This poem was inspired by the Evergreen State;
Washington, U.S.A.
Written one afternoon while
visiting my wife's wonderful family,
Who lives a thousand miles from nowhere, in the foothills,
by a creek.

in//exhale

The mist
Hangs gently in the trees
Like bated breath waiting,
Wanting;
About
To happen.
The air
Smells verdant and alive
Like seed or moment pregnant,
Bursting;
Then,
Here;
It's breathing...

I was toying around with the phrase "in loving memory"
one day, and a thought struck me...
How often do we look back and
see the person we used to be,
and somehow wish that we could
go back and relive those moments?
How often do we look at who we've become
(either by 'chance', or deliberate choice),
and wish we could change it?
How often do we feel as if we aren't really ourselves
anymore?

In Loving Memory of Me

Understanding nothing comes so quickly
Let it slip a few more days again
Then as things begin to show improvement
It all comes flying down around my head
Reaching ever upward through the struggles
These chains can ever bind a weakened heart
Striving for the triumph of a victory
Everything now sees me fall apart
This song's in loving memory of myself
So many pages I have burned
My living memory of taintedness and shame
Shattered by my naked brokenness
I convince myself that nothing's wrong
And that I can heal my pain
I convince myself that I'm so wrong
And I can't forfeit all this mess
I can't forfeit all this mess
Dear God, please save me from myself

We so often settle for whatever's cheap,
without understanding the true cost.
Is it ever really free?

Delusions
(Cheap, Free Pardon)

So heavy on this earth the guilt of all it's done
Rebellion brings it down--
Never will it rise again

How clear a picture does that paint of all we are inside?
Will we ever grasp the things that seem to drive this tide?

Yet out of gloom and darkness
These blinded eyes will see
Out of sin and sorrow
Break this evil's hold on me

Excuses buy the cheap, "free" pardon that we think we
need...

Only...

Paired with division,
It does not accomplish anything.

Delusions of relationship,
Stability,
So cheap
Create in us a fading grip
Of what will kill this flood inside
Of what will stem this hungry tide

Yet out of gloom and darkness
These blinded eyes will see
Out of sin and sorrow
Break this evil's hold on me

The endless battle of our childish lusts and fantasies
Keep dragging backwards from the prize
The life for which we've reached

Yet out of gloom and darkness
These blinded eyes will see
Out of sin and sorrow
Break this evil's hold on me

A bit of a follow-up to the previous poem;
based on the same quotes, verses, lines—ideas.

Escapes

Out of gloom and darkness
Eyes of the blind will see
The essence of humanity
Fallen to its knees
Every part of who we are
Takes its time to fall apart
Watch the moments run on by

As no one,

      Ever,

                  Else,

           Escapes.

Can we ever fully understand
Everything that drives this pride?
Will we ever grasp our part
In this, the endless cycle
Of this mess we're in?
So heavy on our shoulders
The guilt of what we've done
Will we fall and fail to rise;
Or come clean in the end?

I've spent a lot of time over the past year or so wrestling
and seeking to understand
and incorporate this idea of "being" into my life.
The idea of just being still.
Quiet.

Be.

In You We Become

Be.
So short a word it is
And yet
So. Big.
So deep it seems should
Have some length,
Yet, in its brevity lies strength
Just.
Plain.
Be.
No rush, no mess, no hurried pace
No frenzied, panicked, aimless race
Just...
Still, Quiet, Breathe
Only rest
And be.

*I love it when a thought takes root and begins to flow out
onto the paper
as if it's alive and running on its own.
This was one of those moments, where I couldn't have
planned it, or asked for it.
It just came; and there's something inherently beautiful
about that.*

Surely

Surely God is in this place;
Oh, to see Him now...
To reach each moment so convinced
He is here, now, and now
And will be here whenever now is,
On and on until
Now ceases to be now, and then
Becomes then.

Even then,
There He is, then *and* now.
Each moment, and every.
Every moment, God in this place
Each, every, God is there.
All of them, there God is.
There God is.
God is there.
There.
Here.
Now.

God is.

Surely God is in this place;
So peace, my soul, be still
Be still and know that He is God,
That He is God, not I.

Know He is, here and now.
Then and now.
Now and always.

Be still and know that God is surely in this place;
In your here and now.

Be still and know, just *know* my soul,
That God is surely in this place
This place of doubt, this place of fear,
This place of hurt, this place of tears.
This place demanding trust so deep,
So wide and far; a trust so big
You feel you can't...
For fear of stepping out.

Yet oh, how wide! How high! How deep!
How far, how far, the love of Christ!
This love, God is. Our God is love.
Be still and know. Know God is love.
God is.
Love.

Be still and know.
Know He is here, know He is now.
Know no fear, only love.
Be still and know, oh, *know*, my soul
That God is surely in this place
Surely God is in this place
So trust, my soul, and just let go
Let go, be still
Be still and know
Know He is God; just, *only*, know
God is here.
Now.
Always.
Know.
Let go.

I personally find myself so often desiring something entirely
"other"
from that which I know is right, true, and best.
The only thing that sets me straight
in these moments is prayer--
this poem is one of these prayers.

Desire

Why would I find
What my heart is not seeking
Why would I hear
What I'm not listening for
Why don't I want
Things I know I need dearly
Desire of my heart realign

Help me understand understanding
Help me to see what sight means
May my heart come to know with true knowledge
The rush of discovering truth

Why would I desire
What my heart does not yearn for
Hunger
For a food that's unknown
Why would I wait
When all I've done is waiting
Desire of my heart, come alive

I spent a month a couple years ago
—a month of relative clarity in the midst of my depression—
reading the book of Proverbs, from the Bible.
I was struck by so much of the imagery,
and the way in which the wisdom of this book speaks so
clearly.
What follows is a reflection on one days' readings.

Lady Wisdom Cries

The fool in me cries out to she
Who'd set me on this life path:
"Call me naive, but can't you see,
The simple one's the right path."
Then wisdom weeps while walking streets
Crying as she wanders
"How long, how long, oh naive one,
Will your pride be your passionate lover?"

Break me of my ignorance
And teach me what it means to dance.

If nothing but the fear of you can lead to truly knowing truth
Take my simplistic ignorance and turn it into reverence
If I take delight in my own foolish pride
And am willing to throw lady wisdom aside;
Still,
She screams in the streets, finger pointed at me,
Saying:
"This is the reason He died!"
This is the reason He died.
This is the reason I'll die here complacently
Wishing that I would have known

Could
Have known

Should
Have known

       I don't know.

So break me of my ignorance
And teach me what it means to dance.
Take my simplistic ignorance and turn it into reverence.

The genesis of my understanding
Has been in less than centered things
My knowledge based on fool's obsession
And anchored deep in my naivety.

Simplistic, empty ignorance, as stable as it seems
Has prostituted many men, and stolen endless dreams.

So break me of my—take away my—rip out all my ignorance
And teach me what it means to dance...
"How long, how long, oh naive one,
Will your pride be your passionate lover?"

The image of the "prostituted heart" is one that is often run across in the pages of scripture.
While it's not always a pleasant or "easy" picture (no pun intended) for us to take,
it's a pretty clear description of what we do when we forsake The Truth for a lie.
This is another poem that came our of my time in the book of Proverbs.

The Harlot

Wisdom is my sister,
Understanding my intimate friend;
Yet I've estranged myself as a victim,
Far out of reach of their hands.

Cast down from the heights to which I once aspired
Mired in the clay of my own assertions
I'm among the slain due to what has transpired;
Here, you're asking me: "Hey, was it worth it?"

You say that wisdom is my sister,
Understanding my intimate friend;
Yet I've estranged myself as a victim,
Far out of reach of their hands.

The feet of my heart have wandered this town
Flirting with snares that have littered around
The now-flightless fancies of many a man
They're dying around me without a sound

Somehow, wisdom is my sister,
Understanding my intimate friend;
Yet I've estranged myself as a victim,
Far out of reach of their hands.

How can a sister, how can a friend
Really be that when they can't take my hand?
How am I comfortable, how am I free
Facing disaster as the island of me?

So if wisdom is my sister,
Understanding my intimate friend;
I am no longer a victim,
Far out of reach of their hands.

*We were asked to write a prayer of reflection
in response to reading Psalm 139 in a class I took in 2014-
2015.
This poem is the result.*

I've Been

I've been searched and I am known
Even as I'm searching
I've been seen and drawn so close
Even now, I'm learning
I've been scared to let you in
Even as I'm longing
I've been slow to open up
Or hear your quiet calling
I cannot grasp the fullness of
This vulnerability
The mystery of this knowledge is
Too wonderful for me
The very moment I'm laid bare
With nothing covering me
My shame, my intimate-est secrets
Appear to be nothing
I sit, I rise, with you beside
I go to bed, and when I rise
No matter where I go, I find
That you are always there.
I cannot run, I cannot hide
The darkness in me fears
And yet, as scary as it feels,
I can't ignore the light
Drawn by the knowledge I am loved
In spite of all I've done
That I've been formed, crafted with care,
My cells knit one-by-one
This truth I speak, I write, I read,
I preach it to myself, and yet
Because I hold my own thoughts dear
So often I forget

Your love for me, deep as the sea
Fierce as the ocean's tides
Can far out-storm the thunder
Of the hurricane inside
This love, these waters free and deep
And flowing from your side
Pour over me, despite my faults--
The reasons that you died.
It was, at first, my price to pay
And yet, you paid it all
My stitched and moulded, crafted heart
Beats to the rise and fall
Of breath within your perfect lungs
Of blood drawn from your veins
I've been searched and now I know
I'll never be the same.

"We spend a lot of time pounding on the doors that have closed"
--Parker J. Palmer

Closed

Pounding, knocking
Trying, prying
Pushing, pulling, twisting

Grasping, scratching
Yanking, tugging
Shoving now, closed-fisted

Battering and ramming
Punching, banging; anything

Anything but noticing
The open door

Over

There.

"Man never attains to a true self-knowledge until he has previously contemplated the face of God"
--John Calvin

"Tell them that I AM has sent you"
-God

First

I'm learning who I am
Because of the I AM
I guess I never knew before now
That the best way to know myself
The truest way of any
Is by knowing someone else, first.

I have been finding in life that the more
I try to control things,
the more they spin out of control.
The more I try to piece things together myself,
the more they seem to fall apart.

I, Mystery

I love the beauty of a mystery
And yet...
I turn every mystery into a puzzle,
Implying that it has an ultimate solution.

I love the theory of "what if?"
And still...
I'd rather have the answer
Than sit and theorize all day about...

...well...

...Theory.

I love the pregnant expectation
Of fill-in-the-blanks
Fresh pages, waiting, for ideas and words to fill them
But...
I'd rather have the answer key beside me.

Seems to me that all this "I" I've tried to put in mystery
Has turned it into misery instead.

"Then the LORD God formed a man
from the dust of the ground
and breathed into his nostrils the breath of life, and the man
became a living being."
--Genesis 2:7, NIV

Breath

The very breath breathed into me
Inspires to live
Inspired life
This divine air inside of me
it isn't mine
It simply isn't mine

If borrowed breath does fill my lungs
an oxygen whose source
simply cannot be from me--
I can't create it,
Cannot make it,
Can't instate its being
Then where do I get off believing
That sabotage will work;
That lying here in wait for...what?
My own blood—really?
My own breath—truly?
My very life is in my hands...

For a moment of rebellion
I would trade it all?
To gain the world, yet lose my soul...
My life
My breath...
wait, are they mine?

How easily I slip and find
That "me" becomes my energy
My reasons why I live and breathe
I cut the airline and I find
The one I've cut is mine--
The life I've lost is mine
The breath I was so sure was mine was heaven's breath
inside

I have recently fallen in love with the
imagery of closeness and intimacy
God uses when He speaks of how
He longs to relate to His people.
It's extremely anchoring to know that His desire is
to be the center of all that we are.

Inclined

Lean in close and listen
Bend your heart to hear
Turn your ear toward the silence
Let your soul come near

Center all your senses
Everything you are
Root yourself in rapt attention
Listen closely to His heart

I had a bit of fun writing this poem.
While the subject matter is familiar, I think, to many of us,
(the idea of being afraid of silence because it acts as a
mirror to our inner lives)
the words were chosen very
intentionally for a different reason;
In order to communicate a command
to those of us who won't be silent for long enough to listen.
Can you catch the pattern?

Shut Up

Silence, my old friend!
Here we meet again
Understand—there's fear you cause
That keeps me avoiding you.

Usually I'm comfortable, usually I feel strong;
Perhaps if you weren't so quiet, I'd know how to respond?

There is a beauty in simplicity.

Still

Surely,
Serenity equals
Soul
In sync with silence.

It's something we seem to find so elusive, and yet,
it's always right there, waiting for us
to reach out and grab it.
All it takes is admitting that we don't
know, and aren't in control.
Simple, isn't it?

Exist

How can I obtain peace that passes understanding
When my understanding's clouded and my thoughts all seem
so mixed?

But, there—

It's obvious it needs to be beyond my understanding
So outside my comprehension's where this true peace must
exist.

I was struck one night in my quiet time
by the absurdity of our tendency to
play God in our own lives,
and in the lives of others.
When you compare the way we operate,
or even what we are capable of,
against the operation of,
or capabilities of the God of the universe,
we end up looking pretty flimsy in the end.

Juxtaposed

I
I cry
Cry out the pain
Of every
Scar
I
I Bind
Bind up the springs
Of my own
Life.

He
He Roars
Roars out the name
Of every
Star
He
He binds
Binds up the pieces
Of every
Heart.

Why do we run from introspection?
Hide from questions?
Attempt to escape from silence and reflection?
Maybe it's not that we're scared of what God might find--
He already knows everything.
I'm willing to bet that it's because, deep down,
we're scared of what we'll have to admit to ourselves.

Closed Tight

Active awareness
Cannot happen
If I'm afraid of what I'll find
If I...

Open

      up

          my

              eyes.

This is another piece I wrote back when I was sixteen.
I share it because, of my writings from this time,
it struck me as unique in its thought and flow.

Never Live Again

Buried without another chance to breathe
Dead without the choice to truly be alive
Blind without opening your eyes
Deaf without a chance to hear a noise
Mute without speaking any words
Lame without a chance to take a step
Bleeding where there are no cuts
Healing where there are no wounds
Sick without a doctor
A disease without a cure
Eternity with what you wished
While you were still alive
A hell of your own choosing
Becomes now your demise
Lost without direction
Uphill battle going down
Drowning on the firm ground
Swallowed by the sand
Burning on the outside
Shivering within
Falling; never landing
Yet you feel the pain within
Bones shatter with the impact
But they'll never set again
Forced to dwell inside your sin
You'll never live again

I'm somewhat of a closet photographer, and images have always intrigued me,
whether those created with a lens or a pen.
While the idea of photographs is
certainly not a new one in poetry,
with regards to looking at a person's past,
I felt that my 16-year-old self did the idea enough justice to warrant sharing.

Reminisce

Old and faded photographs
Memories of my past
Like all else in this transient life
Things that will never last
Try all I can to save them
Preserve them as they are
But winds of change blow onward
Leaving the good, along with scars
So I sit alone here with my thoughts
Musings wandering in my mind
Pondering the mysteries
I've thus far seen in life
Seeking for the answers
Knowing one place I should look
But my foolish pride takes rule inside
Before long, I've had enough
The replay of the sequel of
These stories in my book
All of them are repeats
Of the ways that I've messed up
Remaking; re-enacting
Replaying worn-out tapes
All-ways running, never facing
All of my mistakes
Carry me away to where my memory will not fade
Walk with me alone and onwards to a better day
Clear my mind of always trying to run from who I am
Help my worn out pictures to
Remind me of you instead.

I'm not sure anymore where this poem came from.
I know I wrote it years ago,
somewhere between the ages of 15-17.
I am intrigued by the refrain: "this place needs work".
How true, of all of us; we who are "becoming".

The Place That Never Ends

So I'm here again
In this place that never ends
The thoughts inside my mind
This place needs work.
An endless trail going on and on
Meandering through my life.
A detour here
No one sees
What's down that road
"The real me"
A roadblock there
Under repair
This place needs work.
No thoroughfare
It seems to carry on forever
Into the distance like an endless river
I have yet to reach the end
Though you'd think by now
I might have exhausted it.
This place needs work.
How far go the reaches of my mind?
What's in there that I still struggle to find?
Do I even know what's down that road--
The detoured route where no one goes?
How do I truly find who I am
And work so I can show to them
All that I was made to be
Longing for escape inside of me
So how do I let it out?
This place needs work.

This one seems to sum it up about right.
I don't know about you, the reader,
but I can often find disappointment to be difficult to take.
The emotional response to the actual emotion
is so often far out of sync with the
actual reality of the situation.
It makes me wonder—are we sometimes more disappointed
in disappointment itself
than we are disappointed with
the situation that brought us there?

Disappointment

Disappointment
Cold
Harsh
Bitter and strong.

Wearing
Wearing
Wearing out
Tying down
Binding up
Painful and unwanted—

A hole in which to trip
Twist an ankle or a knee
And limp the rest of the way.

Stinging
Burning
A void left gaping
Screaming for
What was promised to fill it
Hungry for what it cannot have just yet.

Aching for soothing
Crying for satiation
Disappointment
Breeds in the depressing
Causing bright days to be darkened with doubt
And wishes to remain unfilled.

Disappointment
Never comforts
Never pleases
Never gives
Always takes
Always hungry.

Searching,
Devouring.

Always

Disappointing.

"Those who do not weep, do not see."
--Victor Hugo

Tears

Tears release the tension
Building in my head
But tears refuse to come

Yes, they deny me their pleasure.

To get it out
Let it go
Let it slip
And just know

It's easier within
The refuge of my tears
To let them flow and pour
Hot and twinkling to the floor
Shining streaks left on my cheeks
My worries all dissolved

Tears release the tension
Building in my head
The pain that's caused by many things
So many simple things go left unsaid.

Since moving to a semi-desert climate in 2008,
rain has fascinated me.
I always liked it before, but its effects are so much clearer
on a landscape such as this.
The transformation between the
pre-and-post-rainfall scene is unreal,
and while many have moved here to avoid the rain,
I am always thankful for when it comes.

Rain Today

The rain today inspires me
Instead of dragging my spirits down
The grey-dipped hue the clouds wear now
Says nothing to me of sorrow.
Instead, a vibrance is lent to things
Normally left drab and unexciting.
The verdance of the green, green grass
Is amplified by the glittering drops
The brown hard-wood look
Of aspen trunks
And branches now sticks out.
The contrast of the road and ditch
The green against the black and grey
So bold, yet smoothly blended in
As if it's supposed to be.
The redness of a robin's chest
The song of chickadees in flight
The ripple of each drop that falls
Into a puddle; now it falls
The rain today, Oh, how it falls
Enlightening my day.

Again, sometimes simplicity equals beauty.
And often, clarity comes
with stripping away the peripherals.
I've always been strangely intrigued by the acrostic poem—
But seldom have I created one I'm pleased with.
"Everstill" is, for me, a happy exception.

Everstill

Be
Everstill.

See,
Truly,
I
Lead
Lovingly.

Be
Everstill.

Sense
Trustingly,
I
Love
Lavishly.

Be
Everstill.

Silence
Truthfully
Is
Lusher
Life.

Be
Everstill.

Still
Till
Indwelling
Lasts
Lifelong.

This is another poem—short and sweet.
Its simplicity and brevity speak for themselves.

Glass

Clear as morning
Fresh & new
Unrippled surface flowing
Yet still; always still

I believe in a God who brings a kingdom with Him that doesn't fit the 'norms' of our present reality. The scriptures are filled with seeming 'paradoxes' that threaten to madden those who try to understand them as logical constructs, rather than the beautiful mysteries they are.
Read this poem through the eyes of mystery—it's there the beauty lies.

Paradox

Progress made by standing still
      movement with no motion
Advances made by stances
      silence equals calmed commotion
Real movement earned by rest
      growth by cutting back
Solitude by togetherness
      enough found in my lack.

Wherever you go, there you are...

Shadows

Cold cut and angular
Sharp yet without form
Dark, and yet you're born of light
Changing as you are

There are times where this needs to be an almost-daily prayer in my life.
In its simplicity and brevity, it's possible to use it as such.
I pray this prayer into your lives as well, as you finish this book and rejoin life.

Breathe.

In & Out

Show me how
To breathe release
To inhale pardon
Take in peace
To breathe out worry
Exhale fear
Empty anxiety

Now, and here.

CPSIA information can be obtained
at www.ICGtesting.com
Printed in the USA
LVOW04s1608260416

485379LV00002B/440/P